The Stone Roses were a rock Lancashire, England, UK durii bands of the Madchester mo '90s, their classic line-up compɪɪ>cu vucaɪɪ>c ɪaɪɪ ɒɪ uwɪɪ, guitarist John Squire, bassist Mani & drummer Reni. They issued their breakthrough eponymous 1st L.P., The Stone Roses, in 1989, which was widely praised, many critics regarding it as one of the greatest British albums ever recorded.

The group wanted to capitalise on it by signing to a major label but their original label, Silvertone, wouldn't free them from their contract, which led to a long legal battle that culminated with them signing to Geffen Records during 1991. The Stone Roses released Second Coming in 1994 to mixed reviews, soon breaking up following several line-up changes on their supporting tour, which began with Reni leaving early the next year then Squire during April 1996. Brown and Mani dissolved the rest of the band that October after their appearance at Reading Festival.

Following intense media speculation, the Stone Roses called a press conference on 18th October 2011 to announce that they'd reunited, with a reunion world tour in 2012, including 3 homecoming shows in Heaton Park, Manchester. Plans to record a 3rd L.P. were mentioned but only a couple of singles materialised. Chris Coghill, the writer of a movie set during the Stone Roses Spike Island show of 1990, revealed that June that the group "have at least 3 or 4 new tracks recorded".

A documentary about their reformation directed by Shane Meadows titled The Stone Roses: Made of Stone came out during June 2013. The band released their first new material for 2 decades in 2016, their members touring until the following June, when cryptic remarks by Brown indicated that the group had split up again, as confirmed in an interview with Squire during 2019.

Ian Brown, who was then the bassist & guitarist John Squire, who both attended Altrincham Grammar School for Boys, formed short-lived band, the Patrol, inspired by The Clash, during 1980, with singer/guitarist Andy Couzens and drummer Simon Wolstencroft. They played several gigs that year & recorded a demo tape, but that autumn decided to change direction. Ian had got a taste for being a frontman during the last Patrol show, singing Sweet's Block Buster! to close the set, with their friend/roadie Pete Garner standing in on bass, and Andy wanting to concentrate on guitar.

The band members lost enthusiasm in 1981, Brown selling his bass guitar to buy a scooter & Wolstencroft joining Johnny Marr and Andy Rourke's pre-Smiths group Freak Party. John continued to practice guitar while working as an animator for Cosgrove Hall during the day, while Ian ran a northern soul night in a Salford club.

Squire & Couzens started a new band, the Fireside Chaps, with bassist Gary "Mani" Mounfield, later recruiting a singer named David "Kaiser" Carty and drummer Chris Goodwin then changing their name to the Waterfront, after the film On the Waterfront, their sound influenced by '60s groups & contemporary bands including Orange Juice. Goodwin left before the group recorded their 1st demo, shortly after which John asked Brown to join as singer. A meeting with Geno Washington at a party at Ian's flat in Hulme, when Geno told him that he'd be a star and should be a singer, persuaded Brown to take Squire up on his offer. Ian joined the Waterfront during late 1983, sharing vocals with Kaiser (Dave Carty) for a while.

Like the earlier bands, the Waterfront fizzled out, but Couzens soon decided to form another group, approaching Brown. They decided on Simon, who'd turned down the invitation to drum in The Smiths, as drummer & Pete as bassist, despite the latter saying that he couldn't play anything apart from Block Buster!. They also decided that they needed Chris in the band then when he agreed the line-up was completed.

Leaving their previous groups behind, they only worked on new material, Ian's vocal limitations leading him to take singing lessons for 3 weeks. After rehearsing for some time without a name, Squire came up with The Stone Roses. False stories later emerged stating that the band had at first been called English Rose & that the name was linked to the Rolling Stones, but Brown said "No, I don't know where that English Rose story came from. John thought up the name 'Stone Roses' - something with a contrast, 2 words that went against

3

each other". The group rehearsed for 6 months, while Wolstencroft auditioned for other bands, leaving to join Terry Hall's the Colourfield. They got Chris Goodwin to rejoin, but he lasted for only one rehearsal, so they advertised for a replacement then began auditioning, recruiting Alan "Reni" Wren in May 1984.

After rehearsing and writing songs over the summer, they recorded their 1st demo during late August, making 100 cassettes, with artwork by Squire then tried to get gigs. They played their first show as the Stone Roses on 23rd October 1984, supporting Pete Townshend at an anti-heroin concert at the Moonlight Club in London, Ian having sent the demo with an accompanying letter stating "I'm surrounded by skagheads, I wanna smash 'em. Can you give us a show?". Their performance was seen by journalists including Sounds' Garry Johnson, who arranged to interview them a few weeks later. The group got management offers, with more gigs soon following.

Howard (Ginger) Jones, who'd just left his job as Director & General manager of the Haçienda nightclub, producer Martin Hannett, and Tim Chambers agreed to work with the band on an album, setting up Thin Line Records to issue it, with Ginger taking on management of the group, although they'd already struck a similar agreement with Caroline Reed in London. The band got their 1st positive press during late December, with Johnson tipping them for success in 1985 in Sounds, a feature on the group following during January.

They played their first headlining gig on 4th January 1985, supported by Last Party, after original headliners Mercenary Skank had pulled out. The band's 1st recording session with Hannett took place at Strawberry Studios in Stockport that month to record tracks for a debut single & album. More sessions followed during March, when they recorded their debut single, the double A-side So Young/Tell Me. The group were invited to play a live session on Piccadilly Radio that month for which they first performed a new song, I Wanna Be Adored.

Tony Michaelides, aka Tony the Greek, from the radio station, arranged for 5 local bands to play at Dingwalls in London on February 8th. '85; Glee Company, Communal Drop, Fictitious Names, Laugh and the Stone Roses. Compère for the night was Mark Radcliffe, another Piccadilly Radio DJ. They'd already started to build up a sizeable following in Manchester, their first gig in the North of England, at Clouds in Preston, attracting a good audience, but things descended into a riot after technical problems & friction between the groups on the bill.

The Stone Roses embarked on a tour of Sweden during April, playing their 1st Manchester gig when they got back, at International 1, a venue run by their future managers Matthew Cummins and Gareth Evans. A performance at a warehouse party on 20th July helped to generate more interest in the band then they returned to the studio to record their 1st L.P. in August. However, unhappy with the results & with their sound changing, it was shelved before later being released as Garage Flower, long after the So Young/Tell Me single went out on Thin Line Records that September.

Frustrated by the limited attention that they were getting locally, Stone Roses began a graffiti campaign, with Brown and Wren spraying the group's name on walls from West Didsbury to the city centre, which led to much negative publicity, but increased their notoriety. They began working on new material, including Sally Cinnamon during 1986, but the planned follow-up singles to So Young - I Wanna Be Adored & This Is the One - were shelved.

They split with Ginger Jones, taking on Gareth Evans as their manager, using Gareth's International 1 venue as their new rehearsal space. The band played several UK tour dates, including one at the Mardi Gras club in Liverpool on 11th August 1986, with local promoter and record label owner Ken Kelly & his group Innervision, which several record company executives attended.

As Ian and John began collaborating more closely on songwriting, they decided that they should get a bigger share of income than the other band members, so Alan and Andy left in protest but soon returned. Couzens played an ill-fated gig with the Stone Roses at the end of May before being pushed out by Evans after flying home alone, while the rest of the group returned in their van. Their repertoire expanded that year with songs including Sugar Spun Sister, influenced by The Jesus & Mary Chain and the indie-pop era Primal

Scream, whose Velocity Girl was a major influence on Made of Stone, as they no longer played their older songs.

The band recorded their 1st demo as a 4-piece in December 1986, including the first studio recordings of Sugar Spun Sister & Elephant Stone. Gareth negotiated a deal with Black/FM Revolver early the following year for a one-off issue on the specially created Black Records label. By the time of the release of the single, Sally Cinnamon, the group's sound had changed considerably, with chiming guitar hooks and a strong melody, which alienated some of their old fans, but attracted many new ones. Sally Cinnamon sold out its 1,000-copy run, but failed to have the desired impact.

Pete Garner announced that June that he'd decided to leave the Stone Roses, although he stayed until they'd found a replacement, playing his last gig with the band at the 'Larks in the Park' festival in Liverpool. Rob Hampson took over from Pete, who taught him the bass parts before leaving, but Rob lasted only a week. A longer lasting replacement was former-Waterfront bassist Mani, Gary Mounfield, who played his 1st gig with the group during November 1987. Brown recalled, "When Mani joined it almost changed overnight. It became a totally different groove ... Straight away, everything just fell into place".

Stone Roses played at Dingwalls in London early the following year, a show which was attended by representatives of Zomba & Rough Trade's Geoff Travis, both wanting to sign the band. Rough Trade paid for the studio time to record their single, Elephant Stone, with Peter Hook producing, who was considered to produce an album for them, but was unavailable due to his commitments with New Order, so Travis suggested John Leckie.

The group played a high-profile concert at Manchester's International II in May '88 with James, organized by Dave Haslam to raise funds for a campaign against Clause 28. They tried to usurp James by putting up posters around the city listing the Stone Roses as headliners, also delaying their start to get the headline time themselves and reduce the time that James could play for. The 16-yr-old Liam Gallagher was in the audience, who was inspired to form a band himself, Noel Gallagher having also stated that he was inspired to do the same by attending one of their gigs.

Glaswegian Roddy McKenna, A&R executive with Zomba was also in the audience, who later signed the group to the label, having asked if they could be transferred internally to Andrew Lauder's newly created guitar-based Silvertone Records subsidiary. The Stone Roses were signed to an 8-L.P. deal, buying the Elephant Stone tapes from Rough Trade then issuing them as a single during October 1988.

The band recorded their self-titled debut album at Battery Studios and Konk Studios in London & Rockfield Studios in Wales from late that year into early 1989, produced by Leckie. The first single for Silvertone, Elephant Stone, didn't make much impact, as the group's performances outside the north-west were still attracting small audiences. Made of Stone got more press attention, being picked up by DJ Richard Skinner on his late night Radio One show, but made only UK # 90.

The Stone Roses was released in April / May 1989, initially getting mainly positive reviews, entering the charts at UK # 32 during mid-May. It was followed with the single She Bangs the Drums, which reached the UK top 40, while topping the UK Independent Chart, as they received much more press attention, selling out shows across the country. The band got widespread notoriety when, 1 min. into a live TV performance on the BBC's The Late Show in 1989, the power failed, prompting Ian to repeatedly squeal "Amateurs!" at Tracey MacLeod.

Later that year the group issued a double A-side single, Fools Gold/What the World Is Waiting For, which hit UK # 8 that November. Originally intended as a B-side, Fools Gold soon became the Stone Roses' best known song, a performance of it on Top of the Pops cementing their national fame. It was their first top 10 single, while the L.P. climbed back up the charts to reach # 19 early the following year.

"We're the most important group in the world, because we've got the best songs and we haven't even begun to show our potential yet".

– Ian Brown - NME - December 1989

The Stone Roses' biggest headline gigs of 1989 were to 4,000 fans at Blackpool's Empress Ballroom on Saturday 12th August then to 7,000 at London's Alexandra Palace on Saturday 18th November. The former was released as a live video in 1991 then later on YouTube. They won 4 NME Readers poll awards that year; Band of the Year, Best New Band, Single of the Year (for Fools Gold) & Album of the Year, for their debut L.P. The Stone Roses came to be widely regarded as one of the greatest British albums, although the group weren't happy with the sound on it, Squire describing it as "twee" and not "fat or hard enough".

The band's outdoor concert at Spike Island in Widnes on 27th May 1990 drew a crowd of 27,000, their support acts including; DJs Dave Haslam, Paul Oakenfold, Frankie Bones, Dave Booth, a Zimbabwean drum orchestra & the reggae artist Gary Clail. The show, deemed a failure at the time due to sound problems and bad organisation, became legendary over the years as a 'Woodstock for the baggy generation'. Footage of the concert was issued on YouTube during mid-2010.

The Stone Roses had released their final single for Silvertone 'One Love' by July '90, which hit UK # 4, their last original issue for 4 years, as they began a protracted legal battle to end their 5-yr contract with Silvertone, unhappy with how they'd been paid by the label. Silvertone owners Zomba Records took out an injunction against the group that

September to stop them from recording with any other label, but in May 1991 the court sided with the band, which was then freed from its contract. The Stone Roses signed with Geffen Records, getting a £1 million advance then began work on their 2nd L.P. but Silvertone appealed against the ruling, delaying the record for another year.

After the court case the group separated themselves from Manchester's club culture, spending much of 1992 - 1993 travelling in Europe before starting work on their 2nd album during mid-1993. Progress was slow, hampered by Ian & Squire becoming dad's, along with the death of several folk close to the band. John Leckie left the project as they wouldn't sign a production contract, so the Stone Roses produced the L.P. with engineer Simon Dawson at Rockfield Studios in Wales, where they spent 347 ten-hour days working on it.

The group issued the album, Second Coming, on 5th December 1994, which was mostly written by John Squire, the music having a shady, heavy blues rock sound, dominated by John's guitar riffs and solos. Single Love Spreads hit UK # 2 but Second Coming got a mixed reception from the British press, which music journalist Simon Reynolds put down to 'the resentment that the Roses, divorced from the cultural moment that gave them meaning, were now just another band'.

Reni left the band just a fortnight before a tour in support of Second Coming was due to begin the following March, following a disagreement with Brown, his replacement as drummer being Robbie Maddix, who'd worked with Rebel MC. Session-keyboardist/programmer Nigel Ippinson was also recruited for the live shows, who'd previously played with the Stone Roses on their Chic Remix re-working of Begging You for its release as a single.

A secret 'come-back' tour of the UK was planned for April 1995 but cancelled after the music press had announced the dates, a particularly big blow being the cancellation of their engagement at the Glastonbury Festival that June, because John had had a mountain-biking accident in northern California weeks before the show, breaking his collarbone. The group then organised a full UK tour for November - December '95, all dates selling out in a day.

Squire announced his departure on 1st April of the following year, with a statement that it was: 'the inevitable conclusion to the gradual social & musical separation that we've undergone in the past few years'. Aziz Ibrahim, Simply Red's guitarist on their tour of 1987/88, a former classmate of Pete Garner's at Burnage High School, was recruited as a replacement. The band continued for another 6 months, but there was a deterioration in the quality of its performances after Squire's loss, Ian's voice at Benicassim Festival and the Reading Festival being described as 'so off-key it was excruciating to have to listen'. The music press was united in its criticism, NME describing 'I Am the Resurrection' as 'more like the eternal crucifixion'. Brown & Mani dissolved the Stone Roses in October 1996.

Ian, John and Mani all had successful careers following the group's breakup, Squire forming the Seahorses, who issued one L.P. before breaking up, as well as putting out 2 solo albums. He stated during 2007 that he was giving up music for good to focus on his career as a painter. Brown has released 7 solo albums, plus a remixes and greatest hits collection, all but one of which charted in the UK top 5.

Mani joined Primal Scream as bassist in 1996, staying in the band until the Stone Roses reunited. Reni was largely inactive after the breakup, although he started a new group, the Rub, during 1999, who played several gigs. He said in 2005 that he was writing new songs to perform with Mani. Rumours of a reunion repeatedly surfaced then were dismissed before their eventual reunion. The 20th-anniversary edition of the band's debut L.P., remastered by John Leckie & Ian, was issued during August 2009, including a collectors' box-set edition and the previously unreleased song Pearl Bastard.

After The Sun tabloid published a story on 14th October 2011 stating that the Stone Roses had signed for a series of gigs across the UK, rumours again began to circulate. The NME reported that Alan 'Reni' Wren had responded to the rumours, sending them a cryptic message: 'Not before 9T will I wear the hat 4 the Roses again'. Dynamo told The Sun on 17th October that Brown had confirmed the reunion by saying that the group were 'ready to take the world by storm'

& that he'd sent him the text message 'It's happening'. The following day the band called a press conference to announce the end of their 15-year split.

Brown & Squire performed together live for the first time since 1995 on 2nd December 2011, when they joined Mick Jones of the Clash, the Farm & Pete Wylie at the Manchester Ritz in aid of the Justice for Hillsborough campaign. They performed versions of Bankrobber and Armagidion Time by The Clash as well as the Stone Roses' Elizabeth My Dear. The Stone Roses gave their first public concert since their reunion on 23rd May 2012, playing an 11-song set for 1000 fans at Parr Hall in Warrington. The show, which was only announced that afternoon, was free to attend for those who brought a Stone Roses CD, L.P. or shirt with them.

An 'extensive' world Reunion Tour was scheduled, the highlights of which were 3 homecoming shows at Heaton Park, Manchester, from 29th June - 1st July 2012 then 1 at Dublin's Phoenix Park on 5th July. The Stone Roses said that they'd got plans to record a 3rd album. 150,000 tickets for 2 Heaton Park shows sold out in 14 mins, with the group announcing a 3rd show at the venue on 1st July. They then revealed that a show would take place in Ireland, with Ian saying "After Manchester, Ireland is always next on our list". The 1st leg of the tour began with a couple of warm-up gigs in Barcelona in early June, followed by shows in the Netherlands, Denmark, Hungary, Germany & France.

It was announced via the event's Facebook page on 26th November 2012 that the band would play the Isle of Wight Festival in June 2013. The Stone Roses played at the Coachella Valley Music and Arts Festival on 12th & 19 April that year, having also played at Finsbury Park, London on 7th - 8th June then Glasgow Green, Glasgow on 15th June. A documentary was planned for the group's reunion, with movie director Shane Meadows chosen to film it.

The documentary, titled The Stone Roses: Made of Stone, had its world premiere at Trafford Park in Manchester on 30th May 2013, simultaneously being broadcast live in many UK cinemas before its general release on 5th June. The band announced a couple of gigs on 2nd November 2015 at the City of Manchester Stadium on 17th - 18 June 2016. Another 2 shows were added on 15th and 19th when they sold out, followed by a headline slot at the T in the Park festival on 8th July at Strathallan Castle, Scotland.

The group issued All for One on 12th May 2016, their first new release for over 20 years, with a 2nd single, Beautiful Thing, coming out on 9th June. The Stone Roses announced 3 stadium gigs in the UK on 26th September 2016 - The SSE Arena in Belfast (Odyssey Complex) on 13th June '17, Wembley Stadium in London on 17th June then Hampden Park in Glasgow on 24th June. A couple more dates were added during December 2016, at the Leeds First Direct Arena on 20th - 21st June of the following year. During the performance at Hampden Park Ian told the crowd: "Don't be sad that it's over, be happy that it happened", leading to speculation that it'd be their final concert, which turned out to be the case, as on 16th September 2019, John confirmed that the band had folded.

The Stone Roses' influences included garage rock, electronic dance music, krautrock, northern soul, punk rock, reggae, soul & artists including The Beatles, The Rolling Stones, Simon and Garfunkel, The Smiths, The Byrds, Jimi Hendrix, Led Zeppelin, Donovan, The Jesus & Mary Chain, Sex Pistols and The Clash. The group were part of the Madchester music scene, which mixed alternative rock, psychedelic rock & electronic dance music.

The group influenced other artists, including Oasis, of which Noel Gallagher said "When I heard 'Sally Cinnamon' for the 1st time, I knew what my destiny was". His brother, Oasis' lead singer Liam stated that they were the first band that he saw live and that seeing them perform influenced him to become a singer. Stone Roses' single This is the One has been played before Manchester Utd home matches at Old Trafford since the early 2000s.

The band's relationship with the media was different from others, its members often showing no interest in promoting themselves, as typified by reticent & capricious behaviour. Following the group's reformation in 2011 they still gave few interviews, which confused and irritated many journalists. Their Spike Island press conference of 1990, attended by many from the world's music press, ended in chaos when the gathered journalists thought that the band members were deliberately upsetting them.

John Robb wrote: 'The Stone Roses would stonewall the journalists. With shy guffaws, muttered asides, dispassionate staring, foot-shuffling silences & complete mind-numbing gaps, punctuated by the odd piece of incisive home-spun philosophy from Brown, who occasionally hinted at a well-read mind. There'd be complete silence from John Squire, witty banter from Reni, and Mani spouting off if he let his guard drop'.

However, Robb said that they 'were no fools when it came to the media. One feature of the band's career had been their ability to stay on the news pages of the rock press almost permanently for years on end, including the years when they did f*ck all & they did this by hardly saying anything at all'. Although their reformation conference of October 2011 displayed an elated, talkative Stone Roses engaging with the press, it was followed by total media silence. Other than for Shane Meadows' documentary during 2013, the group gave no further interviews.

Band members

Ian Brown – lead vocals, percussion (1983–1996, 2011–2017)

John Squire – guitar, backing vocals (1983–1996, 2011–2017)

Mani (Gary Mounfield) – bass guitar (1987–1996, 2011–2017)

Reni (Alan Wren) – drums, percussion, backing vocals (1984–1995, 2011–2017)

Pete Garner – bass (1983–1987)

Andy Couzens – rhythm guitar, backing vocals (1983–1986)

Simon Wolstencroft – drums (1983–1984)

Rob Hampson – bass (1987)

Cressa – dancing (1989)

Robbie Maddix – drums, backing vocals (1995–1996)

Nigel Ippinson – keyboards, backing vocals (1995–1996)

Aziz Ibrahim – guitar (1996)

Discography

The Stone Roses (1989)

Second Coming (1994)

Works cited

Haslam, Dave (2000) Manchester, England, Fourth Estate, ISBN 1-84115-146-7

McCready, John. "So Near So Far". MOJO, May 2002

Reynolds, Simon. "The Stone Roses: The Morning After". Spin, May 1995

Robb, John (2001) The Stone Roses and the Resurrection of British Pop, Random House, ISBN 0-09-187887-X

Strong, Martin C. (2003) The Great Indie Discography, Canongate, ISBN 1-84195-335-0

Taylor, Steve (2004) The A to X of Alternative Music, Continuum, ISBN 0-8264-7396-2

After helping generate the fist-pumping soundtrack of a generation, the Stone Roses guitarist John Squire had turned to painting pictures that he'd created on Snapchat. Along the walls of a large concrete box rested big, colourful paintings, ready to be hung. Figures that were lifelike but messed about with, so that bits were in the wrong place, or the background appeared within the boundaries of the figures, like a jigsaw forced together the wrong way.

John said that he started with a photo that he'd maybe found on Tumblr, or taken himself, like one of his wife, at the bathroom basin at home near Macclesfield, which he then manipulated. Damien Hirst had introduced him to the Snapchat collage tool which Squire became entranced with, first as an entertaining distraction, then as a way of creating art. These were produced with the photo editing software Magic Eraser, but it was a similar idea. When he liked what he'd got on his smartphone, he then painted it in oils. Damien had encouraged John to go big, the large space for his show 'Disinformation' being Hirst's Newport Street Gallery in Vauxhall, South London.

"It struck me while I was doing the show & watching the news, I saw there was a parallel between confusing the message figuratively and with regards to information," said Squire. He was standing in front of a distorted, fragmented monochrome guitarist whose face had been obscured by geometric wallpaper. John wasn't sure who the original picture was of: "I don't know if it's a famous person, I'm pretty sure not. It reminded me of posing around with guitars or tennis rackets as a kid, imagining stardom".

Friends since bonding over the Clash at school in Altrincham, Lancs, Squire and Ian Brown had spent much of the '80s messing about with styles & lineups. They'd gained momentum, developing a following before breaking through beyond Manchester with a debut that encapsulated 1989 in vinyl, topping lists of the greatest British albums, having played a big part in the youth of a generation. There'd then been a lengthy gap, fighting with record companies and each other, babies then Second Coming to mixed reviews, more fighting, accusations, allegations, fallouts & walk-outs, the end, solo projects, art … until, after a much longer hiatus, their reformation in 2012, a tour then another ending.

Was that really it for good for the Stone Roses? "Yeah," John said. How were things with Ian? They made a pact when they reformed not to talk about all that, he said. "I'm going to honour that". Would Brown be coming to the opening of the show? "No". Had he been invited? "No". Who was? "I invited Mani, I don't know if he's coming". Squire wasn't keen to talk about the Stone Roses. It was always the same when he was interviewed for a show, he said.

He got asked "A couple of questions about the work then they get down to the serious business of finding out what the scoop is on the band". That was because of their extraordinary enduring appeal, and the pivotal part that they played in the coming-of-age for a generation. How did John see it, looking back through the filter of time? "It was quite a brief period that gets a lot of attention still. I was surprised at the level of support we got when we got back on stage. I don't want to be difficult," he said.

Still pretty lugubrious at 56, Squire often paused before saying something or answering a question, but increasingly they became less awkward. The Stone Roses weren't totally off-limits, music & art having been there over the years, with the painting having come first. His mum had kept a few

21

things that he'd drawn with felt tips as a kid: a polar bear, Greek soldiers, shields and spears. "I didn't really become aware that art could be something enjoyed 2nd hand until punk rock".

Record sleeves? "Yeah & clothes. The paint drips, that was a stepping-stone to abstract expressionism, then 'who is Jackson Pollock?', and I can use this to make my own record sleeves". Which John did, splattering Stone Roses covers with Pollock's influence. He took A-level art at college but failed it, "because I wasn't at all interested in the written work, the art history. This idea that museums were filled with dark religious paintings with a high-gloss finish, it made me feel depressed, reminded me of being forced to go to Sunday school", said Squire.

Was he mostly self-taught, as with the guitar? "I did go to some lessons with a piano teacher. I took him the only sheet music that I could find, which was Rich Kids by the Rich Kids. He tried to play it on the piano but it sounded nothing like the record. I think I had one lesson then realised that it wasn't going to help me get anywhere, so yes, I learnt from books".

John became very good at it, especially on the heavy extended riffs of Second Coming. "Yeah, it's flattering, but I don't think I'm a very good guitar player, or a very good painter. I listen to my guitar playing, my songs, I look at my paintings, I tend to focus on the faults, things that I could've done slightly better." He pointed to a couple of fingers on the manipulated woman in the 3rd panel of the triptych behind him that he wasn't happy with. With more time he would've improved them.

Whether it was a song or a picture, the thrill for Squire was the initial impetus of an idea, rather than the finished result. With a record, "there's so much repetition – because of the recording process, mixing, mastering – the material wears thin by the time it's released".He didn't listen to any of the records that he'd made – Stone Roses, Seahorses, his solo material – but John hadn't given up music. He took breaks from his work in the studio at the farm in Cheshire, picking up his guitar, writing & recording songs. He didn't know what he was going to do with it; only Mrs Squire having heard them.

Did he like working alone? "Yeah, I find it very therapeutic. You're not part of a committee, there's purity to that but sometimes sharing the workload can be a rewarding experience". Apart from the rows, it must've been a laugh being in the Stone Roses. "Yeah, I don't spend much time laughing while I paint". His old group didn't just live on for nostalgic fifty-somethings, their kids were discovering them too, John's own 16-year-old daughter having shown him a picture of her friend getting a tattoo of his own Stone Roses lemon motif:

"My reaction wasn't 'Yay!' I felt guilty in a way, because I knew that they were the same age as Martha". Squire had 6 children, aged from 7 - 26, some of whom have followed similar paths to their dad. His eldest daughter who went to art school, was working on feminist comics. His eldest son was in a band, John having been to see them a few times. "I should go more often, but it's too loud".

What was Brown's idea of perfection? "The Stone Roses!"

Anything else? "The promised land. There's a promised land. The Stone Roses will be there, and sun, sea, sand, fish, monkeys, sex, drugs & Ludo!"

Were they going to manage all that, getting to the promised land? "Yup. None of us are already there. We're waiting for it".

Had anything happened that had surprised or shocked them or had everything gone according to plan?

"Well we didn't have any plans but we've never been surprised or shocked, 'cos when we made a record, we thought it was good and we were really into it, so we thought a lot of folk would pick up on it but we never had a plan, 'cos we do things day to day if we can do. We've never been in a state of surprise . . . or shocked".

Did Ian believe in one love for all folk, whatever they'd done? "Yeah, I do, yeah!" Why? "'Cos it's right. It's one love for all.

You can't have one love but only have these folk in & not those. It's one love for all people!"

Did Brown think that there was enough love in the world? "Not at all, no. I just think that love conquers hate. We're doing our bit, we're trying, we're trying to spread love by making music and playing shows".

Why did they play big one-off events instead of touring around the country? "It makes it more exciting for folk, it makes it more of a night out. You don't just want to play venues that other people play in the traditional sort of rock 'n' roll way, it's just boring. We want folk to have a night out, we want to try to play at different places & we have been".

Did Ian forgive easily? "I forgive but don't forget! I forgive folk for doing things that are wrong, because it's mainly done out of their own ignorance but I don't forget that they've done it. I don't harbour grudges, I don't waste time on grudges, but it's important to always remember what you've seen, what you were and what you know".

Did Brown think that was how to expand one's consciousness? "Yeah, I do, 'cos then you take in more knowledge & that's the way that you become a better person. I'm not knowledgeable enough yet, though".

Was Ian trying to become more knowledgeable? "Always, yeah. That's why you live your life. I read, I speak to folk, I do all the things that everyone else does, and I know that that expands my mind. Travel broadens your mind but so does speaking to people".

Did Brown pray at all? "No".

Did Ian believe in God? "Yeah. I've always believed in something, I just call it God, because it's a term everyone understands. I believe in the forces of good & evil, I believe that they're present in everybody. I think I'm on the side of good over evil, I think everybody is".

Which side was winning in Brown's case? "It's a constant battle. I don't know what part of my character's on the side of evil, I don't look at myself that deeply. I don't analyse my actions at all, I just go with everything. I'm not interested in how my mind works at all. 2/3 of the brain, you don't know what it's there for, so why waste the other third wondering what the rest of your brain is doing? It's better to just go with things".

Did Ian ever wonder why he'd just done something? "No. I'll do that when I'm about 60 or 70. I'll sit back and wonder why did I do all this? Every moment's a live moment isn't it, so it s best to make the most of each one".

Did Brown think about anything a lot? "I think about everything that everyone thinks about: life, relationships, places in the world, things that you want to see, things that you've seen. I want to see Moscow & Africa, somewhere

where you can still see all the animals. I don't like dogs but I am an animal lover".

How far did Ian take his love of animals? Did he eat meat? "Yeah, I eat meat, lots of meat, but there's something about all animals isn't there. I mean monkeys are monkeys aren't they and a cow's a cow & cows are for eating and monkeys are for playing with".

Did he daydream at all? "Yeah, quite a lot. I'm always putting myself on a beach with a lady with some tequila with the sun beating down on me, but other times I want to be out with the Eskimos in an igloo. I like the snow. When I was at school they could never get us back to lessons if it'd been snowing".

Was Brown possessive or selfish? "I'm not possessive but I'd say that I've got a selfish streak. I'm selfish about my time. You're only here once & you should only ever do what you want to do. You shouldn't let folk put you in a position that you don't want to be in. That's always happening, with certain shows people want you to play or certain groups folk want you to support, all things like that but we don't want to do that, we just want to do things that we want to do, 'cos it's our time and our time is the most important thing in our lives".

Was Ian's time to himself really precious to him? "Yes, but I prefer to be with other people. I don't like to be alone".

Did he ever get depressed? "I don't let myself get depressed. I know that I can either think positive or negative, so why think negative, you're just going to bring yourself down, it's a downward spiral. I've felt depressed in the past but I've learnt how to overcome it. John likes being on his own but he's not a depressive sort of person, he just gets a buzz from being on his own, 'cos he likes his own company. I like my own company, but I prefer the company of others".

Did Brown have any recurring dreams? "I used to have a lot of dreams when I was younger about being underwater".

Wasn't that meant to mean being back in the womb? "Is it? Well that's me when I was a kid then. Back in the womb, where it's nice & safe and warm".

Had Ian had any fears of drowning or anything like that? "I did a ouija board once, which said that I was going to drown when I was 35".

Did he think about that at all? "Oh yeah, but if you've got to go, you've got to go, haven't you? Although I wouldn't like to drown".

How would Brown like to die? "Oh, I don't know. In a blaze, just in a blaze".

What'd been the most ecstatic moment in Ian's life so far? At 5 in the morning when I'd been having sex with someone all night but I'm not going to name the person. The most ecstatic moment recently was when I bought the tracksuit I'm wearing at the moment. It's African and it's got Arab writing on the back".

What made him happy when he was a kid? "I was always pretty happy. I don't know why. I guess I was just naturally happy. I know I was quite lucky in that respect".

Did Brown think most folk were happy? "I don't know. I don't know what most people are like".

Didn't he think that most people were unhappy? "It's not surprising, with the country that we live in. There are restrictions on all kinds of things, made by the government, school, all the way through school, it's just the way society is. It's unfriendly, so folk just end up closing doors, keeping themselves to themselves".

Did Ian think things would ever change? "Yes, I always believe things can change, I think it's possible".

Ian Brown & John Squire grew up 2 doors away from each other in Manchester. They 1st met in a sandpit when aged 4. In their mid-teens they decided to form a group, calling themselves The Patrol, with John on guitar, Ian on bass and a couple of other friends, Andy Cousens on vocals/guitar & Simon Wolstencroft on drums.

Brown and Squire moved to another Manchester suburb, Hulme, during 1981, where they met then befriended Johnny Marr, ex-Smiths guitarist & Cressa, who later became their dancer and effects man. Another guy who appeared at that time, who briefly became part of the band years later, was Gary 'Mani' Mounfield. The Patrol changed their name to English Rose, after a track on The Jam's 'All Mod Cons' L.P., but were put on ice in 1982 as John got a job making models for TV animation programmes and Ian was travelling as far away from Manchester as he could get on his scooter.

Brown was hitching around Europe during 1984 when he met a promoter who invited him to play gigs in Sweden. Seeing the opportunity as a free holiday, he returned to Britain to get the group back together, with Ian on vocals, Squire on guitar, Andy on rhythm guitar, a friend called Pete Garner as bassist & recruited via an ad, Alan Wren (Reni) on drums. They chose the name, The Stone Roses, as an amalgamation of their previous incarnation English Rose and rock 'n' roll legends The Rolling Stones.

They started putting on legendary warehouse parties in Manchester where folk could carry on dancing after the Hacienda nightclub had closed at 3.00 am then put out their 1st single, 'So Young'/'Tell Me' in 1985. 'Sally Cinnamon' was issued on FM/Revolver during 1987 then Pete Garner left to be replaced by their old friend Mani on bass. The Peter Hook-produced 'Elephant Stone' was released the following year, with John's distinctive artwork gracing the single's sleeve for the 1st time.

Early the following year, the band went on tour, playing to 12 fans in Cardiff & 10 in Hull. Their next single, 'Made Of Stone', reached the Top 100 that March '88 in the independent charts then in May, their self-titled album was released to much critical acclaim. The first single 'She Bangs The Drums' entered the UK charts at # 36, as Stone Roses played the Blackpool Empress ballroom that August, which was then their biggest gig.

'Fool's Gold'/'What The World Is Waiting For' soon hit UK # 5, as the group appeared on the same edition of Top of the Pops as Happy Mondays, with their gig at London's Alexandra Palace selling out weeks in advance. They made their 1st live TV appearance on The Late Show, blowing all the BBC fuses after 45 secs of 'Made Of Stone', which they played too loud. FM/Revolver re-issued 'Sally Cinnamon' in January '89 then the Stone Roses wrecked their offices with cans of blue and white paint after the label made a video to accompany the single without their permission. They played to a crowd of 28,000 during May at Spike Island, while their long-awaited single 'One Love' became a big hit.

Stone Roses were already putting their own after-hour shows together by 1985, way before the Blackburn rave scene & all-night illegal parties. Returning from a riotous tour of Sweden the band wanted something more exciting than playing the same old venues around town. Their manager Steve Adge had the idea of finding their own 'private' venue to play after attending all night shin-digs down south. Hiring an old British Rail warehouse behind Piccadilly station they named it The Flower Show, to put the authorities off.

Tickets included a telephone number to ring for directions, together with hand drawn maps and word of mouth, punters making their way down a dark uninviting block to find Manchester's 1st ever warehouse party. Taking to the stage at about 1am with all members dressed in black the Stone Roses launched straight into 'Heart on the Staves' then never looked back, putting in a sinister but energetic performance that went down a storm with the crowd of skinheads, rockers, party-goers & general music fans, being such a success that the Flower Show part 2 was staged a few months later.

The anti-clause-28 gig at the International during '88, a benefit gig against the Tory party's policies on the homosexual community, went down in Stone Roses history as the first of the break-through shows that sent the group on their way. The night was also important for the Gallagher brothers who were in crowd. Noel met The Inspiral Carpets guitarist Graham Lambert after enquiring about a copy of the gig that he was trying to tape, while Liam pictured himself up there doing the same thing after seeing Ian Brown's stoned swagger working the stage. He started his own group showing the roots of Oasis, coming straight from that night at the International.

It' also remembered for the headline act James being stood-up. With both bands capable of headlining the event, it was James who took top billing- being the more established. Stone Roses were due on at c. 10pm, but when the time came for them to take to the stage they couldn't be found, which kept James waiting then playing to an emptying house. Over the years its been understood that the band put off their slot till as late as possible to finish in time for the last buses of the night while grabbing the headline spot, whether intended or not that's exactly what happened as the group put in another memorable performance.

Still having a punk edge they showed their poppier, cooler side that night, which reflected the Second Summer of Love and it was there that the epic Stone Roses set list was first played, starting with their old song 'I Wanna Be Adored' then ending with the outstanding 'Resurrection'. It was the night that Manchester looked up, took notice & hailed the band.

The group played over 30 dates across the UK for 3 months of the spring/summer of '89, climaxing at the Empress Ballroom, Blackpool, on 12th August. A traditional venue that hosted early Rolling Stones and Beatles gigs in '64, Brown said of the Stone Roses' reasons for playing the north's favourite holiday destination; "We wanted to play Blackpool to give folk a day out, when you live in Manchester there's nowhere else to go, it's the local seaside resort".

It was the height of the house revolution with E driving things along, the borders between dance music and bands having crossed over, a unique time. A night described as the ultimate Stone Roses performance, it was a show etched deeply into the band's live history, marking the point when they really put themselves & Manchester on the map.

Back then an independent group pulling in a crowd of 4000 meant that there was more out there than Stock, Atkin & Waterman, something was definitely happening. Thanks to the same crew who shot TV music show, The Tube, Blackpool is probably the best ever Stone Roses performance on tape, and although the event was one that you had to be there to fully appreciate, watching it back it was clear how special & influential their live set really was.

Their 1st major London show was held at Alexandra Palace on 18th November '89, playing to 7000, the band's biggest crowd to date. Like the 'Happening's of the late '60s Ally Pally hosted a full on event, being more a statement than a great live performance, as the night's also remembered for the poor sound quality, with the sound hitting the back wall then bouncing back, so there seemed to be a delay. This marred it but couldn't hold the Stone Roses back from playing their most renowned London show. The video of Ally Pally, although of quite poor quality, is the only live recording on the net, featuring Reni's backing vocals on She Bangs the Drums.

Big outdoor events arrived during the summer of '90, with Spike Island. After a short tour of Scandinavia the group touched down in a space between Manchester and Liverpool in the chemical industrial town of Widnes to a crowd of 30,000. As a rock show Spike Island didn't really work but cemented the guitar/dance cross-over that defined an era. It was a celebration of arriving, marking the point when the band became the most important of their generation.

Although once again the Stone Roses were fighting against the sound, because the rig wasn't really up to the job, it was never going to stop them playing a blinder, being sent on their way to the Belfast & Glasgow Green shows with a fire that produced some of the group's finest live moments.

Both shows saw The Stone Roses hit top gear with Glasgow being a personal favourite among the band themselves.

At Feile festival, the classic Second Coming gig, held at Cork City's Gallic Athletic Association stadium 'Pairc Ui Chaoimh' in '95, the group shared a bill with Paul Weller, Ash, and The Prodigy, whose set broke down twice due to power cuts, while Kylie Minogue performed on one of the smaller side-bar stages. There's not much by way of reviews or footage but at a Stone Roses press conference at the Soho Hotel one October Mani said "See that Feile show in '95, that was probably one of the greatest shows the Roses ever played, 2nd behind Glasgow Green in my humble estimation".

3 men stood on a man-made island in the Mersey estuary one grey Thursday morning during January '90, deciding that it was as good a place as any to make history. They'd been scouting locations for a massive outdoor Stone Roses show for the previous few months, visiting quarries, speedway tracks & caravan parks around the UK, but none of them had seemed quite right for what they had in mind.

Concert promoter Phil Jones recalled, "It was Gareth Evans who came up with the idea of Spike Island. It was near where he lived and they'd had events on there in years gone by, so myself, Gareth & Roger Barratt, who ran a company called Star Hire and who'd already agreed to do the staging, went out there, took a look around then said, 'Yeah, we can do this here'. The council were there, we'd already worked out what the capacity would be & we all shook hands on it that afternoon".

For a band who'd once stated their wish to play a show on the moon, a reclaimed toxic-waste dump seemed an unlikely staging post, but that was always part of Spike Island's appeal. The group could've had their pick of venues, such was their popularity at the beginning of the '90s, even Knebworth, where Pink Floyd, Led Zeppelin and The Rolling Stones had played, but they had no interest in following in the footsteps of others. As Ian said in 2010, "We wanted to do something outside the rock 'n' roll norm & do it in a venue which had never been used for that sort of thing before. This was back in the days of raves, remember. We started out doing warehouse parties and we still had that mentality where we wanted to play different venues. We wanted to play places that weren't on the circuit".

Spike Island certainly wasn't, but while Heaton Park, scene of their Manchester reunion shows of 2012, was bigger and the band members would probably say that Glasgow Green, where they played a month later, was better, Spike Island was the Stone Roses' defining statement, a celebration of not only their own success, but of an entire youth culture. As Mani said "It was a gathering of the clans. We were always confident that if we just turned up, folk would come. That was always the way it was with the Stone Roses. We knew what we'd started, we knew the reactions we were getting all around the country & we just wanted to get everyone together".

The group were a bridge between the past and the future, between '60s psychedelia and the burgeoning acid house scene. They'd arrived towards the end of Thatcher, the vanguard of a new sound, a new style & the latest drug, ecstasy. Brown spoke of killing Queen and becoming bigger than The Beatles & briefly both seemed within the realms of possibility. "History in the making was how it felt at the time. It'd been hyped up for months before; endlessly emphasised that this was the defining moment of a generation – when rock meets rave, the point at which the music world was going to explode in one big group hug", wrote Andy Fyfe of the Spike Island show.

Anticipation reached fever pitch as May 27th got closer. The Stone Roses hadn't played live for 6 months, with no-one sure when they would again, because a criminal damage case brought against the band by their former label boss, whose office, cars and girlfriend they'd daubed in paint as retaliation for a 'Sally Cinnamon' video that he'd commissioned against their wishes, meant that the threat of prison was hanging over their heads. However, they escaped with a fine.

Meanwhile, a short warm-up tour of Scandinavia hadn't gone according to plan, with the press conference held the day before the gig verging on calamitous: BBC & ITV news crews refused to cover the event when Gareth Evans tried to charge them for access, while the surly, uncommunicative band was accused by a journalist of "treating these people like f*cking sh*t".

When the group arrived on-site – not in a helicopter but in a rented minivan – they weren't impressed by the heavy-handedness of the security and lack of facilities. Brown stated during 2010: "The organisation was shambolic. The PA wasn't big enough for a start, and certain things were going on that we didn't know about. The management were taking folk's sandwiches off them at the gate to make them buy 5-quid burgers when they got in. Some kid got impaled. He broke out of jail, tried to jump the railings then ended up leaving his bollocks on top of them. We were still finding out about this stuff 2 or 3 years later".

Mani added "Our management really f*cked up. There were security guards taking booze off people, there was a lot of overcharging for food & drink, and there weren't enough facilities on-site. There were a lot of aspects of Spike Island that were really badly thought out, but none of that is the band's job". However, Phil Jones disputed their version of events: "What you have to remember is that Mani doesn't like Gareth, and he also has a very limited idea of how these things work. We provided exactly what the council told us we had to & if he went through the paperwork, he'd see that Gareth complied with everything. There's no blame to be apportioned, and certainly not on Gareth – if anything it was Widnes Council. Do you think Mani went wandering around the site to find out how many toilets there were? He arrived in a vehicle, went backstage, played the gig then went home again. He had no idea about the number of toilets".

The site presented environmental challenges, the island having only one access point, requiring the construction of new bridges, and as flat land surrounded by water, it was exposed to strong gusts of wind coming in off the Mersey estuary. Jones' immediate concern was a rising tide that briefly threatened to put a stop to the whole event. "I was stood on the stage with the deputy chief constable of Cheshire, Widnes division, who told me, 'It's a spring tide, Phil. It's never gone over this island before, but it is getting very high. If it goes past a certain level, you're going to have to get everyone off'. It was a high neap tide on a full moon, which is the highest tide you can get. It never came close in the end, but that was the worst moment".

After a supporting bill that included DJs Dave Haslam, Paul Oakenfold & Frankie Bones, along with sets from a Zimbabwean drum orchestra and reggae artist Gary Clail, the group took to the stage shortly after 9pm, with Ian urging the crowd to "Do it now, do it now", as 'I Wanna Be Adored' rumbled into life. As 30,000 fans suddenly rose in unison, a cloud of red dust formed in front of the stage, triggering asthma attacks among some members of the crowd. Others got caught up in the moment – Shameless actress & Eccentronic Research Council member Maxine Peake, who was 15, recalled "being completely overwhelmed when they came on. I started to get hysterical, and I couldn't breathe. When the woman behind me asked if I was all right, I had to pretend to have asthma, because I was so embarrassed. It was ridiculous".

A camera crew from Central Music TV were there, but at the last minute the band told them to stand down. The only footage of the gig was shot on a fan's camcorder, with those who were there seemingly unable to agree on whether the performance was 2nd rate or sublime. Andy Fyfe recalled them playing "abysmally. Colleagues who went to the soundcheck the day before said it was amazing, electrifying, they were on top form, but from what I recall, they had no funk to them at all. There was a certain weight of expectation that they didn't live up to".

However, author Jon Ronson wrote, 'Even though the sound was blowing all over the place, it was impossible not to be moved by it. When Brown came out brandishing an inflatable globe, it was everything it was supposed to be – the world in their hands. When you saw it, you absolutely felt like you were a part of something, at the centre of that place & time'.

Phil Jones said "Take it from me, folk could hear the gig fine. There were 30,000 people there, and 29,990 of them had a whale of a time. Whenever I read about Spike Island, it's always negative. Show me firm evidence that the sound wasn't good & the lights were the best f*cking lights I'd ever seen. What we had on that stage was state of the art. We didn't scrimp on the PA either, but the council wouldn't allow it to go above a certain decibel level".

It was all over 90 mins later. Paul Oakenfold said "I touched base with the group in their dressing room afterwards – I think that everyone involved felt a sense of triumph that day. They were great musicians with a great sound who came along at the perfect time – sometimes timing is the most important part of it. By the time they got to Spike Island, there was a whole movement that they were at the forefront of: You had what was going on in the clubs in London, and what was going on up north with bands like the Stone Roses

& Happy Mondays. The whole country wanted a change, and the Stone Roses captured that at Spike Island".

However, for Mani, "It all felt a bit anticlimactic. I wasn't overly happy with the way it had been thrown together & there were a few incidents that pissed me off. We went back to our manager's nightclub in Manchester after the show, and the snide c*nt tried to charge us for a can of lager, after we'd made him that much f*cking money". The group themselves made nothing from the show, but they made history.

Outdoor shows on that scale have become commonplace since then – Oasis at Knebworth, Blur at Hyde Park, the Stone Roses at Heaton Park – but none loomed so large in the collective consciousness as Spike Island. It was a real moment in time, the beginning of a long hot summer when England nearly won the World Cup again, the height of a period when Manchester & the north-west of England felt like the centre of the universe.

Jon Ronson wrote, 'It really felt like an 'us versus the world' moment, because of the amateurism of the organisation as much as despite it. It didn't feel to me as much like the start of something as the end of it – the ideal place to bring down the curtain on what it'd been. The record had been out for a year by then and because the Stone Roses didn't release another record for so many years afterwards, it framed perfectly the summit of what they'd become & what they meant to folk'. A quarter of a century on, it was a summit that few bands have ever come close to scaling.

The Stone Roses were 4 lads from Manchester who thought that they could be better than the Beatles. They had influences, but they wanted to be individual, because only then could they be longlasting, meaning something to future generations. They survived and shone because the group wanted their debut L.P. to be a timeless record. Listening to it took many back to baggy, to Madchester, to ecstasy, dancing in fields in floppy hats & flares but the album also existed in its very own space.

Sometimes it was cool to be arrogant, OK to be confident and cocky, the band having cheek & ridiculous self-belief. When producer John Leckie finished work on their eponymous debut, he told them that they were going to do well. They shrugged; they knew it, having that idiosyncratic Manc swagger, epitomised by Happy Mondays before and Oasis after them.

Although Ian Brown was handsome, with his pale northern skin, Mick Jagger lips & hollow cheeks, the Stone Roses were also very much a group. One got the idea that when Ian and John Squire went into the studio with bass player Gary 'Mani' Mounfield & drummer Alan 'Reni' Wren, they trusted and understood one another, being able to do what came naturally to them. They didn't worry about the influences of Jimi Hendrix or Johnny Marr, they just wrote what was in their hearts. You can't create genius; it just is.

When The Stone Roses was issued in May 1989, it soon became a classic. The opening chords of 'I Wanna Be Adored' were a perfect statement of intent, sending shivers down the spine with a rumbling, thumping bassline before Squire's immense guitar sound set in. It mattered not that the lyrics had little more than a dozen words; the sentiment was crystal clear. Leckie's clever production allowed the band to explore their ideas, leaving the songs with raw edges, making them feel real rather than synthetic. Brown's vocals were assured although sometimes a bit croaky, silky smooth yet a little cracked & the folky Simon and Garfunkel feel wasn't just present on the 59-sec 'Elizabeth My Dear', an attack on the Queen set to the music of 'Scarborough Fair', but throughout the L.P.

In some ways it wasn't the sound of Manchester in the ecstasy-fuelled late '80s, but a universal sound born of the '60s. Squire experimented with Hendrix on 'Shoot You Down' and Marr on 'Bye Bye Badman' but preferred trippy, psychedelic guitars, knowing how to write anthems, from the magnificent melody of 'Waterfall' to the closing track, 'I Am the Resurrection'. Ian said that he had to coax the group into letting the latter run to its full 8 mins, 12 secs, as they didn't want to be seen as pretentious prog rockers.

The others had concerns about freeform jamming, while Brown was wondering what might become of them: "If we do get big ... we're either gonna get f*cked up or we're gonna die - that's what happens to everybody". Ian wanted to be in the biggest band in the world, thought he was, but knew there could be serious consequences, although he didn't anticipate a long fight with their record label, delaying their 2nd album for over five years .

The Stone Roses split up very publicly, the stories seeming so important back then, with Brown & Squire no longer speaking, paint thrown over the offices of their record label but 15 years later what really mattered was the art, their music. The group had northern cool but they also had northern soul. They believed they should matter, which they did.

At the Reading Festival of August 1996, the pop world was waiting for perhaps the most important British group of the past 10 years to come onstage, but The Stone Roses were no longer really with us. There was a 'Stone Roses' on stage, but it was without 2 key members and most of the romance, soul, magic & mystery associated with the name. What was happening on that stage marked the end of an era. Ian Brown was singing in a bellow that may've sold a few papers in a crowded city centre, folk being shocked into leaving, some in tears, as the Stone Roses were falling apart before their eyes.

When Ian was singing 'The past was yours but the future's mine' to a captivated generation 7 years earlier, it had seemed as though the Stone Roses heady trip wouldn't end. From '89 - '90, they were the most influential, far-reaching thing to happen to British rock music since the Sex Pistols, their effortless blend of melodious chimes and hard-edged funk transforming British culture. They looked different, with stylish inelegance, heralding outsize baggy jeans & trainers chic, while being up front about drugs. They arrived on-stage to the rumblings of acid house, a 1st for a rock band, piercing the nation's heart with a debut L.P. that soon shifted 500,000 copies, later topping Best Albums of the '80s polls, The Stone Roses being regarded by some as the greatest ever.

However, while many groups, including The Charlatans, Blur, The Verve, Primal Scream, The Bluetones, owed a lot to the Stone Roses, with Noel and Liam Gallagher forming Oasis after seeing them, perhaps their greatest legacy was that their music & attitude rescued British rock. Pop was in a state of post-Live Aid disrepair during the late '80s, being musically and socially impotent. Perhaps as a reaction against the excesses of stadium rockers including Simple Minds, 'credible' bands began to disappear from view, wary of success then along came The Stone Roses, declaring that they wanted to be on Top Of The Pops, wouldn't rest until they had a chart-topper, stating that they wanted to be as big as Michael Jackson.

Once the pop world had heard Fools Gold & Made Of Stone, it decided that songs that good should be hits, the Stone Roses restoring ambition to rock, helping the likes of Happy Mondays, Inspiral Carpets and Ocean Colour Scene to blossom. They rejected an invitation to support The Rolling Stones, having refused to perform on The Wogan Show until they were interviewed by the man, because they wanted to pull his wig off.

They didn't really need anyone's help, the media tagging the Stone Roses/Happy Mondays/Ecstasy phenomenon 'Madchester', after the Happy Mondays, 'Rave On: The Madchester EP', but the group wouldn't co-operate. Their legendary cool indifference to selling yourself came out of a gang mentality rooted in scooter days & years of struggling around Manchester but they just knew that they were better. The band had the best drummer in years, Alan 'Reni' Wren, along with a great bassist, Gary 'Mani' Mounfield, whose notes flowed so beautifully on Made Of Stone. Then there was John Squire and Ian Brown, one of the best songwriting duos since Lennon / McCartney & most potent guitar/vocalist couplings since Mick Jagger and Keith Richards.

John & Ian had grown up together, their friendship being almost telepathic. Squire was very quiet, but his evocative guitar-work spoke for him. When he did mumble something Brown often finished his sentences. John was practical and creative, his Pollock-esque splatters adorning the Stone Roses' album sleeves. Ian was razor-sharp, with a strong sense of justice; a street-lad & former punk rocker whose heroes were boxers and civil rights campaigners, having traveled widely & read The Crossman Diaries and The Bible. He wasn't a gifted vocalist but his nasal whine expressed romance & authority.

Brown's songs contained religious symbolism eg. 'I Am The Resurrection', there often being something worth hearing when he spoke. His offhand remarks including, "It's not where you're from, it's where you're at", became catchphrases and ideals for Stone Roses believers. Where did it all go wrong? The seeds were sown during their 5 year hiatus from 1990 - 1995, when the group were involved in court cases, as well as the protracted recording of Second Coming.

When they returned, they did so with a much darker, disturbed Led Zeppelin-esque rock sound, some great new songs, including Love Spreads, Driving South & Ten Storey Love Song, but soon lost founder member Reni, who left on the eve of their live comeback in March 1995, amid unsubstantiated drug and money rumours. The Stone Roses had lost their impetus, having been jinxed. First Squire fell ill then broke his collar-bone just before the postponed headline of Glastonbury during June '95, with shows being erratic, Ian's voice getting a lot of criticism, a series of disappointments leading up to John's acrimonious exit in April '96; the debacle at Reading signalling the demise of the band. Squire then had success with the Seahorses, Mani joined Primal Scream, with Brown making a much anticipated solo comeback.

Ian looked like a bona-fide rock god during '97, his hair only being slightly shorter than at Reading the previous year, his clothes those of a snowboarder & his expression that of a wee boy who'd just been given a Christmas present. His eyes were dark and alert, his cheeks sunken due to his simian bone structure. "Oh the beard. Been growin' it for a week. It's for the video (for his latest single, My Star). Half way through, I 'ave to shave it off, like I'm reborn".

What was Brown's earliest memory?

"Aged 4, laid in some grass, just chatting with a girl & being told I was 'bad' then being taken out of school".

What was Ian's family like?

"Poor, down to earth. My father was a joiner. He looks like me. I've got a younger brother and sister. I grew up in Warrington, which was grim but fun".

Who was his first hero?

"When I was a kid, there was no-one bigger for me than Mohammed Ali. I can see that '74 Foreman fight as clear as a bell & I got all the books. My walls were covered in Ali and Bruce Lee pictures then later it would've been the Pistols".

Legend had it that Brown met John Squire in a sandpit, at the age of 4.

"There was a sandpit in the fields near our house. He remembers me being naked, but I don't know if that's right.

We became friendly at 13 or 14, when we were put in the same class at secondary school. I started chatting to him & I took God Save The Queen, the first Clash L.P., and 'One Chord Wonders' by The Adverts round to his house. He was into The Beatles & The Beach Boys, but he only had compilations. I played him these punk records then a week later he'd bought the Clash and 'God Save'. He went mad about the Clash after that, following them all over".

What attracted Ian to John?

"We were total opposites. I was very outgoing, the kid that would stand on the table in front of the class doing impressions of the teachers. I was the class joker & he was the loner. He got out of sports so he could do art. I think he was the 1st kid in the school to play truant, and he did that by himself but at 13, 14, we'd walk the streets together & sit in each other's bedrooms playing records.

He got his guitar when aged 15. The first thing he learned to play was 'Three Blind Mice'. Then he'd play his guitar for me when I went round. He's a funny kid. I know he's really, really quiet and doesn't speak to anyone, but when he was with me he'd never shut up. Everybody knows him as a man of few words, but in those days he was garrulous with me, definitely. I did spend a lot of my life & a lot of the Roses' life talking for the kid. I knew him so well that I'd finish his sentences off but then in the end that didn't happen".

Was it Squire's guitar that made Brown want to be in a band?

"No, I didn't want to be in a group! I was more interested in going off on my motor scooter to Northern Soul all-nighters. In Manchester, you couldn't avoid Northern Soul. Also, I did karate from 11 to 18. Aged 14, I was teaching it at weekends to grown men. I wanted my own karate school but John was getting good on guitar. He'd formed a band called The Waterfront with Andy Couzens (later of The High) on rhythm guitar, Mani on bass, a kid called Kaiser singing, and Chris on drums.

John kept pestering me to sing, so in the end I went to rehearsals with me & this Kaiser kid singing. We called ourselves The Patrol. We had a song called 'Come On'. 'Come Aaaaann!'. We played a few youth clubs but I didn't really get anything off it. Anyway, later I was at this party in Hulme, my mate's roadie-ing at Salford University, and he brought Geno Washington down to the party, a superstar kind of guy, big personality, all over the room. He came up to me then he said 'You're a star. You're an actor. Be a singer'.

I remember him on the street smoking a big spliff when this copper came round askin' 'What are you doing?' He was blowin' his spliff in the copper's face, that was '83 & he was goin' 'I'm Geno, man. GENO. GENO!, singin' the Dexy's song, really cool. The copper didn't do anything, he just walked away. A few weeks later I was thinking about what the guy's said. What did he mean, I'm a star, an actor? Anyway, I thought we'd give it a go, so we kicked Kaiser out then started the real thing, The Stone Roses, in March '84".

What was the original Stone Roses line-up?

"Me, John, Pete Garner, Andy Couzens, and we found Reni from an ad. There's a story that we were called English Rose, but that's untrue. Mani didn't join until November '87 but we were mates then also. Finding Reni was crucial. John was a punk guitarist when we met Reni, but Reni could play anything. He'd been brought up in pubs, so he'd practiced & practiced on his kit and played with proper pub entertainers. He had a musical talent that none of us had. We all had to graft & work, but he was born with it. Pete Townsend saw our 1st gig (Rock Garden, 1984) and said that he was the best drummer he'd seen since Keith Moon".

Did Ian rehearse for stardom in front of a mirror?

"Well, when you do karate, you train in front of mirrors, so I'd always looked in mirrors. A few Ali moves. I never stood there with a tennis racquet".

The early Stone Roses were very ragged. They didn't seem to reflect their musical vocabulary – Northern Soul, say?

"No, but we also liked The New York Dolls, still do. John, Andy & Pete were very into Johnny Thunders, Reni was into Van Halen. He'd never heard reggae when we met him. He'd been brought up in east Manchester, which was more heavy metal. He was into Thin Lizzy and AC/DC. He was a proper rocker, used to go to Donington. We used to rip the piss out of him but we were very enthusiastic. We just wanted to make a noise".

What was Manchester like back then?

"There was no-one about. There was The Smiths, New Order. I liked a few singles, but there wasn't anyone giving you a charge. We loved Slaughter & the Dogs. In 1985, we worked with Martin Hannett (issuing neglected single, So Young, on Thin Line), because he'd made 'Cranked Up Really High', not 'cos of Joy Division and all that Manchester heritage, but Hannett was in a bad way. We caught him snorting coke off the 'There's no-one quite like Grandma' gold disc! He was a junkie; lovely man, but nothing else mattered.

Manchester was very important to us though, because we'd play to 2,000 then we'd go to Liverpool, only playing to 30. We played our own gigs under a railway tunnel. That's what a group should do, innit, play an illegal party in the middle of the night. The police would be outside & the promoter would give them crates of beer. They didn't want to close it, 'cos there were too many people. Different days really. We were isolated in Manchester but that made us more determined, because in those days they'd say to make it you had to move to London, go to all the parties, get your face about. The Smiths had moved to London, which disappointed us. We believed we could do it from Manchester, we stuck by that and we did".

When did they meet Gareth Evans, their manager?

"We'd seen an advert in the local paper during 1986, so we went to see him. I think we'd been in the room 2 mins when he said, 'This is what I do' then he dropped his trousers & he'd got these underpants with an apple on the side. 'Pommies' they were called, and he was dealing in 'em". We thought he was crazy, but funny. We got on well with him. We thought he was Al Capone & he thought he was Al Capone too but we wanted that kind of guy, a Frank Dileo, so we clicked straight away. Plus, he owned the International clubs, so we could rehearse there for free and watch the bands for free, which we did. We saw everybody who played the Internationals from '86 to '89".

Was the group's sound evolving?

"Yeah. At 1st we had lyrics & choruses, but they weren't proper songs. Then by c. '86 or '87, me and John started working more closely together. We'd write a song on an acoustic guitar then take it into the rehearsal room, whereas before we'd just all throw out what we had. I was listening to Prince, Far I, loads of black music. There was this tune called 'War on the Bullsh*t' by Osiris, which I used to play all the time, along with The Beatles, Pink Floyd, Hendrix & Love's Forever Changes. John used to buy Mary Chain and Primal Scream records, but we didn't. Andy Couzens went then we started to shape songs. When Mani joined in '87 that made us more musical, because Pete the old bass player wasn't musical enough. John & Reni had improved. I'd improved but Mani was the final piece of the jigsaw and everyone around us knew it".

54

Did they steal the tune for Made of Stone from Primal Scream's 'Velocity Girl'?

"No, I'd never heard it. John probably had, but he won't have ripped it off, because this is what used to get me about Oasis at the start. Me & him used to write loads of songs, but they'd be Beatles songs. We'd go, 'Oh sh*t, it's 'I Feel Fine" or 'Sh*t, it's Daytripper' then we'd sack it. Whereas these lads would just go with it. A long way!"

When did the Stone Roses' classic songs start to appear?

"c. '88. We started recording during May/June, having signed the deal with Silvertone in April then we'd written Bye Bye Badman, Shoot You Down, Elizabeth My Dear. We wrote most of that 1st album in the few weeks after inking the deal, 'cos we'd blagged the record company. We told Silvertone that we had c. 30 or 40 songs, but we only had c. 8. We'd scrapped loads of songs. We'd had I Wanna Be Adored since '85 but it used to be at breakneck speed then we slowed it down. The turning point was getting Waterfall in the set, a song about a girl who sees all the bullsh*t, drops a trip and goes to Dover. She's tripping, she's about to get on this boat & she feels free. Waterfall was the first time we went 'Wow, this is it!'".

The Stone Roses released their classic debut album during May, 1989, revolutionising the scene. The sound of music changed virtually overnight, with an upsurge of groove-orientated guitar bands influenced by them and a host of older hands following their lead, including Primal Scream, with Loaded. Youths wore loose-fitting clobber and Kangol hats, a la Reni. When the Stone Roses & Happy Mondays appeared together on Top of the Pops that November it was a generation-defining moment, a high watermark for pop. They recorded 'The Stone Roses' with John Leckie, who'd worked with XTC, Magazine, Simple Minds but wasn't the name producer that he later became after Cast, Radiohead and Kula Shaker. Why had they chosen him?

"Cos we nearly signed to Rough Trade, and Geoff Travis recommended John Leckie. We heard the Dukes of Stratosphere (XTC offshoot) L.P. that he did. It was like the sounds of the '60s, so we thought he must be really clever to get those sounds".

What could Brown remember about the album sessions?

"Pure fun. Proper good times. We were in London, recording at night. We'd all get a taxi back at 7 in the morning & we all shared a house on Kensal Rise. We were skint, they'd give us £10 / day for food, which was a load for us. We started in Battery then we went to Conk Studios then finished it off in Rockfield in Wales. After 4 years on the dole, suddenly you're in a country studio with someone cooking for you and a bag of weed in your pocket. Yeah, great".

Had they known how good the L.P. was?

"When we'd finished recording, Leckie came up to us to say 'Listen, this is really good. You're going to make it'. I remember thinking 'I know'. It could've been even better. Mani & Reni didn't get their thing down as heavy as it was in rehearsals. I think Leckie had listened to Waterfall and thought it sounded like Simon & Garfunkel, so he turned the bass and drums down. He'd gone for that Byrds, '60s thing but Mani was the best white bass player that I'd heard, so I wish that was more audible on the record".

Were they quite druggy at that time?

"When we were young we took speed then c. '86 we started smoking weed. I haven't touched speed since. In '88 we started taking E's, trips we'd done c. '84 or '85. By the time the trips came in in '88, we'd done ours years earlier. Before, I was aggressive onstage, I used to walk round the crowd singing in people's faces, high kicking, or kiss someone's girl, wind someone up, but later I'd become more mellow. I think it was the music. I never took any drugs before I went on stage. I never smoked any weed & I've only ever done one show on E. I don't drink, I've never touched beer since I was 18. It was totally natural".

Was the relationship between ecstasy and the Stone Roses overplayed?

"Definitely. With us a lot of the drug stuff came from Gareth Evans back then. We never even smoked in front of him, but he was just trying to be a rock manager, trying to make us notorious. I remember that first review in the NME: 'They make Levenshulme sound like a district of San Francisco' & 'They're psychedelic, but they're '60s'. It was just an average review but the following week I was in Spectrum in London when this journalist came up who'd reviewed the album.

He said 'What are you doing in here?' then the week after that we were their favourites. Once they found out about ecstasy, that's when they started writing about us. I watched them all go on Es. Last time I saw Alan McGee he said 'I remember you cracking up laughing at me, you and Mani stood in the corner. At the time, I thought you were judges but now I remember it was because I was stood in the middle of the dancefloor with my fists in the air to Phil Collins' In The Air Tonight!'".

The press were very slow to champion the Stone Roses. Almost uniquely in the modern era, the press discovered the group after the fans.

"Definitely. They wrote about us 'cause they had to".

The tour of April-May, '89 was one of the greatest pop tours of all time.

"A big thing was happening in England at that time with ecstasy & we arrived at exactly that time. I felt great, righteous. I felt we were pure, that we weren't conning anyone. We were real and beautiful".

They sounded euphoric, sensitive, focused on records, but in interviews they came over as surly, it having been suggested that they adopted a stance given to them by Gareth Evans, who'd said 'I gave the Stone Roses their mystique'.

"It's b*llshit, that. I never wanted to be no whore or desperate. The easiest thing to do is get your nipples out. I never wanted to do that. When we said we were the greatest, I believed it. We never consciously put an act on – we just never felt the need to sell ourselves, because we knew we didn't have to but, yeah, I didn't suffer fools gladly. One or 2 journalists who came along were quite bitter, cynical. They didn't come with anything positive, so they got nothing from us".

As the band became bigger, they stopped touring in favour of huge, one-off events like the 'days out' of Blackpool & Alexandra Palace.

"We wanted to make things special for our fans, give them a whole day of experience. Blackpool was fantastic, but Ally Pally wasn't what it should've been. We used a friend who was a sound engineer, but he'd never done anything anywhere near that massive. The sound was poor. After the show, me and John left in a car & didn't say anything for 2 hrs but we were smokin' at the time. We'd written Fools Gold. At the end of '89, we had our pictures taken at the top of a mountain. We were on top of the world and it felt like it".

How important to the group was Fools Gold?

"The thing is, we had a drummer with soul, so we always had a beat. That's what made the Roses".

Ian was expressing self-doubt in interviews by early '90, casting aspersions on the fickle nature of pop music.

"Maybe I was worried because it was all getting too much. We were getting things like 'These are 4 Jesus Christs' & I wanted to keep it real. That was the hardest thing for me: 'Don't worship me' but it's impossible; if you refuse someone an autograph they get upset. Everyone misinterpreted 'I Wanna Be Adored'. It never meant that I wanted to be adored. It was a song about sin. I never personally gave a f*ck about being adored. The star was the audience. I wanted, and I still want, to finish the days where folk are looking up at Bono or whoever. It's a reaction against that pampering, limousine, coked-up thing. We wanted to kick over those icons".

Were the Stone Roses very close at that time?

"Oh, yeah. We lived in each other's pockets. We were so tight at the time that we had our own language. No one could get near us. Gareth was the closest, but he couldn't get in. We were close on every level. Everybody wanted the same thing".

The 'One Love' single was a mistake.

"I agree. The chorus wasn't strong enough. We tried for an anthem. We wanted to cover all bases but ended up covering none".

The Spike Island 'mega-gig' the previous month had also been a bit of a fiasco.

"We had a w*nker [Gareth] running it. We trusted him. We're not the kind of people that put on a show where folk have their sandwiches taken off them at the gate. That reflects on you, 'cos the kids think 'Oh, they're doing that'. The way folk were treated on that day was despicable. The sound wasn't good enough 'cos he didn't spend enough money on the PA. Another thing, we never helicoptered into Spike Island. There was a chopper, but it wasn't us. We got a bus!"

Were they very naive, business wise?

"It wasn't that, we just weren't going for the dough. I used to say 'If we all end up in a mansion with a pool each, we've achieved nothing, so what? So another 4 kids got rich. It doesn't mean anything. We've got to change the music business, we've gotta change the world".

One revelation at that time was that they weren't being paid royalties on CDs.

"Yeah & 90% of what we did was on CD! Criminal, isn't it? I mean, originally we'd recorded 'Elephant Stone' for Rough Trade but then Silvertone/Zomba came in with a longer, 8-

album deal, so that's why we went with Zomba. Everybody praises that 1st L.P., but we never had one royalty cheque from it".

They couldn't trust the record company, but they couldn't trust their manager either, because he'd got them that deal. It must've felt like they were being shot at from both sides.

"Yeah, that's why we sacked Gareth Evans during '91, who sued. We were doing more time in courtrooms than in studios but we had to win the case against Zomba otherwise we'd have ended up on the dole, 'cos our pride would never have let us record for Silvertone again. There was even talk of making our own bootlegs but the court stuff did bog us down & as a unit we became separate. I was down in the courtroom every day, but they were all in Manchester. We got our dough [by signing to Geffen] in 1991, but John moved to the Lake District. So, yeah, that's when it started changing".

Caught up in litigation, the band made sporadic forays into the recording studio between court cases, but all wasn't well. For reasons that have never been fully explained, the group didn't issue another record for 5 years.

Were things falling apart within the band?

"Yeah. We did Fools Gold and One Love to a drum loop & Reni played over the top, so now John's got no confidence in Reni. All we ever hear is that Reni's the greatest drummer anyone's ever seen, but we've got a guitarist who doesn't want to play with him. He wants to play to loops. Eventually, Reni was turning up at the studio going, 'What the f*ck am I doing here?'"

That must've destroyed Reni?

"Bitterness crept in, but in a way Reni got enjoyment, because he thought that John would have to come round. He never did. When Reni left the group, John never phoned him up. He hasn't laid eyes on him for 2 years. He's said in interviews 'Oh yeah, I've seen him', which Reni's blazing about. So yeah, that was the start of the decline".

John Leckie said during 1993 that they "spent 2 years looking for a new sound but came back to where we started". A typical day's 'recording' would consist of the engineer setting up a drum loop but then nothing would happen.

"Yeah. We weren't a band. It was the John Squire Experience. I let it happen, because I thought we had 3 or 4 albums to follow but there were ego problems. I knew it got his goat when the press said 'Ian Brown's boys' – and you'd go to the shows where everybody's got Reni hats on. A girl'd send me a Jackson Pollock book then he'd go 'That should be for me'. I thought, 'Ok. He needs attention, I'll let him get it out of his system'. We've got plenty of time ahead of us".

Squire was writing heavily Led Zeppelin-influenced material by then time but both Brown & Mani said that they "never liked Led Zeppelin".

"We're in the studio, and for me those 3 [John, Mani & Reni] are the best players to come out of England but they're sat around watching Led Zeppelin videos, going, 'Wow, look at that' and I'm watching them watching Led Zeppelin, thinking 'You're all over these guys. They've not got that funk, they've not got what we've got. I thought, 'Don't they realise where we are in history, who loves us? We were better & bigger than Led Zeppelin. We weren't trying to be them old blues guys".

Was it a loss of self-confidence, due to being cocooned in the studio, each day getting further away from the Stone Roses 'phenomenon' & their adoring fans?

"Yeah. It's simple for me. John Squire didn't know who he was. He didn't know who the Roses were. Looking back, he never realised the love that folk had for us".

Was Squire changing as a person?

"Definitely. He became more insular. There was only me could get in his front door. Simple. Reni's knocking on his door but John's hiding behind a chair. Then once he's cut me off – c. 1992 – that's it. We used to go off on writing trips to Scotland, but suddenly he's going on his own. He cut himself off. I carried on writing my own things but he refused to work on anyone else's stuff. I went along with it 'cos I thought it was temporary. Mani? John wrote all his basslines. Mani was happy – at that time – to do what he was told. Mani's going into the studio, putting down some unbelievable things down but Squire's going "No. You're doing this here".

It was a myth that they were lazy.

"I've never spent all day in bed".

Wealth had made them lose their sense of urgency.

"We never had a load of money. We only got £100,000 each, which I gave away to my family within 3 days. The rest of the Geffen advance went on recording equipment, wages & tax".

One day Brown walked around Manchester with £100,000 in a holdall, giving out wads to the homeless.

"It was a carrier bag".

John told The Face during March '95 that he'd had a cocaine problem during the making of Second Coming. He said that November, "The reason the L.P. took so long was because there were too many drugs in the studio".

"He was on cocaine all the time, so he's speaking for himself. A man's got cocaine up his nose, he's not saying anything to anybody. You're giving nothing if you're on coke, all you're doing is taking. Of course there were too many drugs in the studio. He's got coke up his nose, that's the end for me. If you're on coke, you're busted – there's something the matter with you".

Squire also said "The group were on different drugs at the same time. It can be destructive if everybody's on a different plane".

"Yeah. I smoked weed. You'd have to ask Reni what he was on, and Mani was on everything".

Why did Ian think that John succumbed to cocaine?

"Dunno. Easy to get – you're in a band, you get the best gear. You start off using it to bolster your confidence. You're insecure but then you can't go out without using it. You're using it in the studio, you're using it at home. Pick the phone up, the next thing 4g are arriving, so you shut yourself in your room, you never come out. I'd go away for a week, come back and no one's talking. He's not talking to him, he thinks he's a dick & he thinks he's a dick, and I'm trying to be the daddy of them all. I'm walking in each room & getting big hugs, but he won't work with him. Charlie is the devil, simple as that".

The Stone Roses re-emerged on November 21st, '94 with their biggest ever hit, UK # 2, Love Spreads, followed by the musically darker Second Coming album. However, Reni left the group on the eve of their March '95 comeback tour, the catalyst for a sequence of events including live triumphs at Feile and Wembley, the departure of Squire plus the ignominy of Reading '96.

Had Ian expected Reni to go?

"Yeah. Because of the situation, he wanted to leave to spite John, but he didn't want to do it to me. I'd considered leaving myself, in 1993. It was no surprise to me when Reni left".

As no reason for Reni's departure was given, rumour spread that it was either due to arguments over dough, or that he had a heroin problem.

"No one had a beef about money. If we'd delivered 50 songs, we'd have shared £20 million".

When the band began touring with new drummer Robbie Maddix in Oslo on March 29th '95, they put up a united front.

"We were feeling closer, Robbie came in, who was fired up, full of beans. He learned about our past & became a full-on member. He fitted perfectly".

At that time it seemed as though the knives were out for them in the music press; perhaps rooted in their decision to give a comeback interview to The Big Issue.

"The press were upset. We got letters, but we wanted to use our position to make dough for the homeless".

Another decision that backfired was giving reviewers copies of Second Coming on the day of its release.

"Maybe we were niave, but we just wanted kids to have the same chance as a journalist. We weren't worried what the press would think. I seriously thought it was a great L.P., I didn't expect a bad review. One journalist wrote that it was crap; 6 months later, he told me that it was his album of the year".

What were Brown's memories of the '95 world tour?

"We were erratic. We were poor in Copenhagen, but by the time we got to Japan we were smokin'. I think the Australian shows were some of the best we ever did, and some of the late '95 gigs in England. I think the all-nighter at Brixton that December was the best we ever did here. We were gutted about not headlining Glastonbury [due to Squire's broken collarbone in a cycling accident] but we could see the future. We'd acquired a keyboard player [Nigel Ippinson] who was musical. We were getting tight again. People were there for us & we were feeling better again".

Were they talking again?

"No. There were 2 coaches on that tour. One was a coke coach and one wasn't. There were 16 on one & 5 on the other. John travelled with the coke coach. He'd say 'I travel with the crew'. Bullsh*t! He travelled with the coke, 'cos he couldn't take coke in front of us, 'cos we wouldn't have it. All the way through that tour we wanted to smash coke but he's a grown man, you stop preaching to folk about coke".

When did Ian's relationship with Squire reach rock bottom?

"The kid had cut himself off. When Philip Hall [Stone Roses publicist who'd just agreed to manage them] died, John wouldn't come to the funeral. I said 'At least show his mother and father that he meant something' but no, he wouldn't come to the funeral. The 1st rock of civilisation is when they bury the dead. I knew that there was something the matter with the kid then. Nobody enjoys funerals, but I thought differently about him that day. I thought 'Little f*cker'".

A turning point?

"Definitely. I thought he was the most selfish coward".

If Philip Hall had lived to manage the group things would've been different?

"Who knows? In this business, he was one diamond man. He'd have been good for us, no doubt. I don't think we'd have got into the messes we got in. We didn't have a manager & we were open for anyone to have a poke".

Had Brown felt overshadowed by Oasis, who'd taken their blueprint.

"It didn't get me down. They're from Manchester and good luck to them. They're not my thing, although I'm glad that someone saw us then formed a band. At least they became the biggest but I've never had to put coke up my nose to go onstage or in a studio, so I can be proud of that".

They ended '95 in triumph at Wembley, but on April 1st '96 John Squire quit. Was Ian surprised?

"Definitely. I thought we'd be recording during April then playing the festivals in the summer. It was a complete surprise. John never once said that he was upset. He never said a word. We'd done over 180 shows around the world & he never once phoned anyone else's hotel room".

Was Squire aware of his increasing isolation?

"Of course, but coke doubles isolation. In fact, he won't have been thinking anything clearly but when he phoned me up at home that night he said 'Ian, I can't do it. I'm a phoney'. I said 'Can't do what?'. He said 'Play the guitar anymore'. I phoned him back in a couple of days then said 'I waited for you all them years'. I went to see him but he wouldn't open his door. He didn't have the courtesy or the bottle.

Next morning, he flew to London for a press conference. Suddenly, he'd 'just found' a group, a management team and a solo deal. Yeah, sure you did. It was a surprise. I'd been phoning him through February 'cos we'd written 6 songs. He never phoned me back. I thought he was busy. Was he f*ck! He was sorting out the rest of his life. He's quite happy for some fat Hollywood guy to give him a schedule for the rest of the year, but I wasn't, 'cos that's not what the Roses were about. Is that all he wants to be, a pop star?"

By the time of the last Stone Roses shows, Brown's singing was getting pilloried in the press while John was being proclaimed as the last guitar hero.

"Yeah, 'The Unforgettable Squire'. He read that & believed it. 'I'm doing it all on my own'. That's one of the last things I said to him, 'Do it yourself'. That's what he's done – surrounded himself with 3 buskers, a little Elvis, and he's pay-rolling them to kiss his arse, although I notice he's already managed to squeeze out 1 drummer".

Were the criticisms of Ian's voice justified?

"Yeah, sure. I'm not the world's best singer, but when you're onstage stood in front of 4 Fender Twins & you've only got a little monitor, you try singing. When I was onstage, I wasn't allowed to have my voice coming through the side, because he didn't want to hear a voice. He's got his 4 guitar amps turned up to 11, I've got a speaker that big and I'm struggling to stay in tune, because I can't even hear anything. I've got films of those shows. He's not playing with no group, he's on his own, but I still think the shows were great".

Had there been any communication between Brown & John since he'd left the Stone Roses?

"No. I saw him on Good Friday last year. He was in his Range Rover when I saw him. To me, he looked like someone was on the floor with a gun at his head".

Why did Ian carry on the band after he left?

"I wanted to finish the mystique and be real. I thought with Aziz & Robbie fired up we could bury our history. Yeah, we managed that at Reading".

Why was Reading such a travesty?

"I didn't go to bed the night before, like a dick. We'd played 5 shows in Europe, we'd been getting better at each one. I saw Cressa [original '89 Stone Roses dancer and 'vibes man'] the night before & I went on the piss with him, smoking weed all night, I was so excited. Normally I don't drink. No powder, no. I haven't touched powder since '90 but I must have f*cked me voice. At the time, I didn't realise that it was all going wrong. From the stage, I couldn't see anyone crying or leaving but later, when I heard the tape, I knew that I sounded terrible. It was a cabaret version".

The group fell apart 3 weeks later. The final statement that Brown released seemed very bitter.

"Why was it bitter? I said 'Having spent the last 10 years in the filthiest business in the world, it's a pleasure to announce the end of the Stone Roses'. It was a pleasure and it is the filthiest business in the world. There were other problems. I got paid £9,000 in '95. We made £1.2 million on the road but it disappeared – partly 'cos Evans was suing us & we were paying lawyers, and partly 'cos folk in the camp got light-fingered. At the end, I was glad to get out".

Ian put out his debut solo album, Unfinished Monkey Business during March, 1998, an eclectic, funky record which reaffirmed his status as one of the unmistakable voices of British pop. That month there was a slice of tuneful psychedelia, My Star.

Why had Brown decided to return?

"I'd seriously considered gardening. F*ck it, everything I'd believed in was finished. John had left me. Me best mates were robbing money off me. I had summonses up to here. I didn't want to know any of it. F*ck it, I'll do gardening for old folk but then I was going out & kids were coming up to me asking 'When are you doing something?'. In the end, I thought I probably should, so I spent last winter holed up with a bass, an acoustic guitar and a drum machine, learning audio techniques to add to the things I'd picked up over the years. The first song I came up with was Lions on the acoustic. I thought 'I can do this'".

From the lyrics to Lions, it seemed that Ian had considered quitting England?

"Nah, I got the idea from the England-Germany game. I thought it was pathetic, grown men crying. Years ago there was a religious programme on BBC2, in which they had a dread answering questions about his faith & as the credits went up, this dread's beating his staff going 'There are no liiions in Inglannd'. Why do they have lions in Trafalgar

Square and on the England shirt? There've never been any lions here".

What was the origin of the title, Unfinished Monkey Business?

"When the Roses had disappeared, recording Second Coming, the press were desperate for any stories of what we were up to. The drummer from Dodgy told this Guardian journalist that I was making everyone call me 'King Monkey'. I thought it was really funny".

Was Ian wary of getting involved in the music business again?

"I wanted to avoid it. In the end I paid for the record myself, finished it then said to the company [Polydor], 'Here it is'. I sold it to them rather than let them pay for the recording & have them telling me what to do. I said 'Look, I've got no band, I'm not planning any live shows. This is it'. A week later it's, 'Where's your group? When are the shows?' so there will be shows, probably in March".

Who played on the L.P?

"I couldn't have done it all myself. I'm not a virtuoso but I play bass, acoustic guitar, keyboards, drums, harmonica, and a trumpet. Then there's Reni, Mani, Simon Moore, a brilliant drummer, Aziz, Nigel [Ipinson, keyboardist with the '95-'96 Roses]. I live near Warrington & I've got carpets all over my walls and an 8-track in my bedroom. I've got the buzz now, I'm writing all the time".

Aziz, guitarist at Reading, formerly with Rebel MC) had come into his own now that he wasn't playing someone else's parts. His slightly Asian-flavoured playing on Unfinished Monkey Business was innovative.

"Aziz plays on 6 tracks, he's co-written 4. He's perfect for me, because he doesn't drink, he doesn't take drugs & he'll chat".

Mani and Reni played on Can't See Me, an amazing groove that saw them finally picking up the gauntlet that the Stone Roses threw down with Fools Gold. How had that come about?

"It's a DAT that I had from '95 of Mani and Reni. I play bass over the top of it. I phoned them up to ask 'Can I use it?' – & they were cool. There's every possibility that we'll play together. I was jamming with Reni last week. He's now singing, playing guitar. In '95, me and him were in New York when we saw this kid playing drums on Times Square. Reni was looking at this kid & he knew the kid was better than him. It gutted him. He didn't pick up his sticks for a year but now he's playing drums better than ever. He's got big hair and a beard & I call him John The Baptist. Can't See Me is my favourite, yeah. Very fresh. We never followed up Fools Gold, because John never rated it. He felt embarrassed to play the funk".

The stuff that he'd recorded since with the Seahorses was far more traditional. Was he always the most traditional member of the band?

"Yeah. He can't stand reggae, doesn't like Bob Marley".

Brown had a song, Ice Cold Cube, which was played at Reading in a different, inferior form. What was it about?

"Ice Cold Cube was Reni's nickname for John".

Some of Ian's new lyrics were the most vitriolic that he'd ever sung 'You're a social chameleon, change to suit the people around you' from Corpses; who was that about?

"I didn't write that one. That's about girls who hang around folk in groups for cocaine".

The single, My Star, referred to 'NASA corrupters'. Was that a continuation of the overlooked Stone Roses political side?

"I see it more as social comment than politics. I've always been principled. I was brought up that way. The song's just pointing out that we have these wonderful space programmes, but they're mainly used for military purposes. It's vitriolic, but positive as well".

Brown had previously cited Martin Luther King and Rosalie Parkes as figures that he admired. Who'd impressed him lately?

"Anyone who can overcome their own enviroment & the lies that we're fed. Rappers from Jamaica who can uplift folk".

Was Ian impressed by Tony Blair?

"No, he's ineffectual. Like, now there's a chance to get rid of fox hunting. For the 1st time in history we've got 'em but he's stalling. There's other things that I disagree with – curfews on 14-year-old kids, forcing kids to work for their dole. Blair's got a massive landslide, the Tories smashed themselves and it was beautiful, but there's nothing to replace it. All the folk who suffered through the '80s. Blair wants to be everything to everybody, but he'll end up being none of them. He's still kissing the arse of business & they're still attacking single mothers on welfare. I voted Labour, but if we'd had Arthur Scargill's Socialist Labour in my constituency I'd have voted for him".

How did Brown feel in himself lately?

"I feel good. Focused".

He'd always been guarded, so how come Ian was being so open?

"I don't have to cover anyone's back now".

Was Mohammed Ali right to go for his last tilt at the heavyweight title?

"With Leon Spinks? No, he was badly advised. He carried on too long. He didn't know when to stop. Do I know when to stop? Definitely. I've got at least one more L.P. inside me".

Brown – singer, groover, rebel and The People's Prince – walked through the streets of London with his new Mexican girlfriend. As his eyes glistened in the moonlight, he turned to reveal the Mexican translation of the name, Ian Brown. "It means born winner", he whispered.

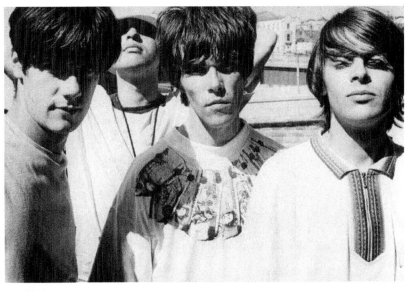

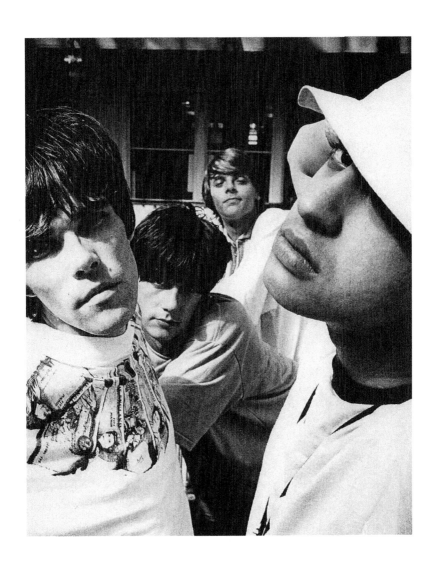

122

127

144